Meet a Baby Koala

Jon M. Fishman

Lerner Publications ◆ Minneapolis

For Mom, who saved my stuffed koala at the fair

Lerner Publications Company
A division of Lerner Publishing Group, Inc.
241 First Avenue North
Minneapolis, MN 55401 USA

For reading levels and more information, look up this title at www.lernerbooks.com.

Library of Congress Cataloging-in-Publication Data

Names: Fishman, Jon M., author.
Title: Meet a baby koala / Jon M. Fishman.
Description: Minneapolis : Lerner Publications, [2018] | Series: Lightning bolt books. Baby Australian animals | Audience: Ages 6–9. | Audience: K to grade 3. | Includes bibliographical references and index.
Identifiers: LCCN 2016037240 (print) | LCCN 2016047891 (ebook) | ISBN 9781512433838 (lb : alk. paper) | ISBN 9781512450569 (eb pdf)
Subjects: LCSH: Koala—Infancy—Juvenile literature. | Koala—Life cycles—Juvenile literature.
Classification: LCC QL737.M384 F57 2018 (print) | LCC QL737.M384 (ebook) | DDC 599.2/5139—dc23

LC record available at https://lccn.loc.gov/2016037240

Manufactured in the United States of America
1-42019-23889-10/12/2016

Table of Contents

Tiny Baby

A baby koala grows inside its mother. The baby grows for about thirty-five days. Soon it will be born.

Koala mothers give birth alone. Koala fathers don't help care for their young.

A baby koala looks very different from its parents. It has no fur. It can't see or hear.

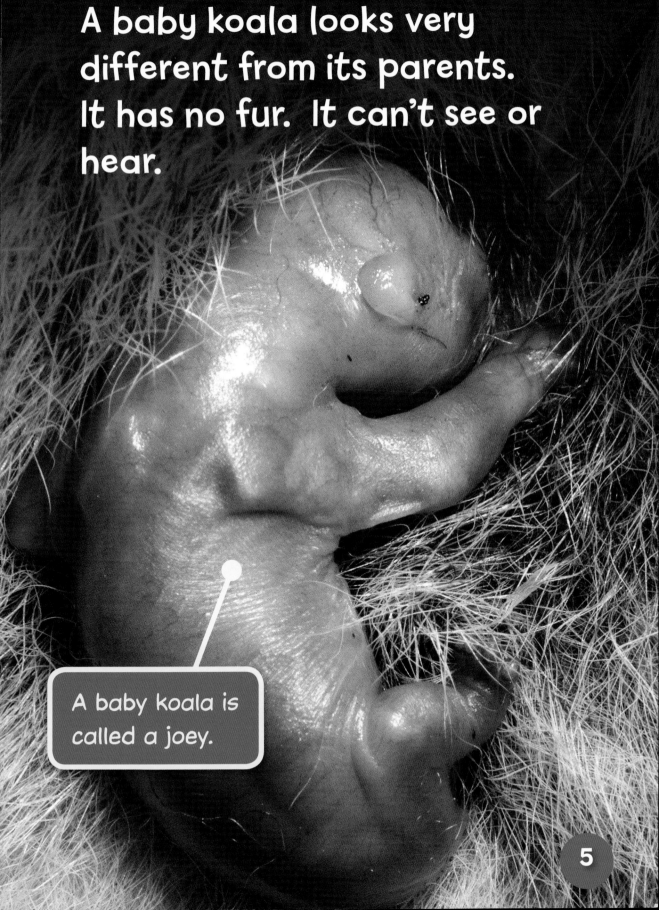

A baby koala is called a joey.

Joeys are about 1 inch (2.5 centimeters) long when they are born. They weigh less than 0.03 ounces (1 gram).

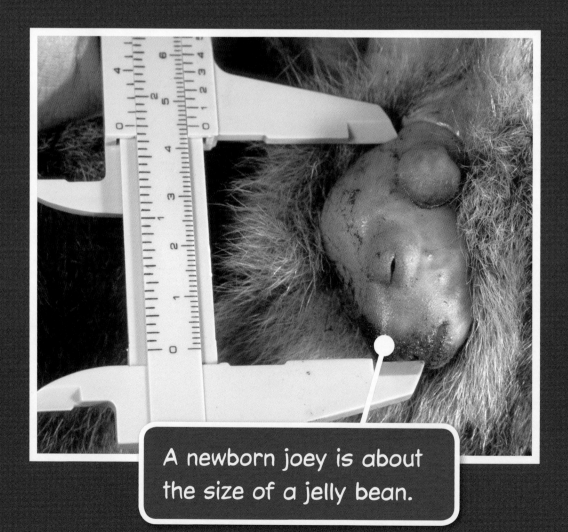

A newborn joey is about the size of a jelly bean.

The joey is much smaller than its mother. An adult female koala usually weighs 9 to 20 pounds (4 to 9 kilograms). That's about the same as an average bowling ball!

Mom and Joey

A joey crawls to the pouch on its mother's belly right after the joey is born. It goes inside. It stays there and grows for the next six months.

The joey drinks milk from its mother inside the pouch. The milk helps the joey grow strong.

Mother koalas protect their joeys from predators such as birds and snakes.

Then the joey starts spending time outside the pouch. It clings to its mother's belly. It rides on her back.

A joey weighs about 1 pound (0.5 kg) when it first leaves the pouch. A large grapefruit also weighs about 1 pound.

Koalas spend most of their lives in trees. Joeys learn to climb.

The sounds a joey makes change as it grows. It learns to bellow.

Yip-yip! A joey calls to its mother. She goes to her joey when she hears the cry.

Food from the Trees

The joey keeps drinking milk. It also drinks a substance from its mother called pap.

A joey eats by grabbing leaves and pulling them into its mouth.

The joey starts eating leaves after spending a couple of months exploring outside the pouch.

Koalas eat mostly leaves from eucalyptus trees. The leaves are tough. Pap from its mother helps a joey digest eucalyptus leaves.

A one-year-old joey weighs about 4.5 pounds (2 kg). That's similar to the weight of a 68-ounce (2-liter) bottle of soda. The joey is usually too big to fit in the pouch.

Koalas rarely drink water. They get most of their water from their food.

Home Alone

A mother with a one-year-old joey may soon have another baby. Then the joey leaves its mother to find its own place to live.

Some joeys stay with their mothers until they are about two years old.

Koalas live alone. They bellow and growl at times to keep other koalas away.

A joey usually won't go far. It looks for a home in the trees near its mother.

A female koala can have her own babies when she is two or three years old. Males are usually four or five when they have babies.

Male koalas bellow to attract mates when they are ready.

Koalas in the wild may live between thirteen and seventeen years. These creatures are one of Australia's best-loved animals.

Koala Life Cycle

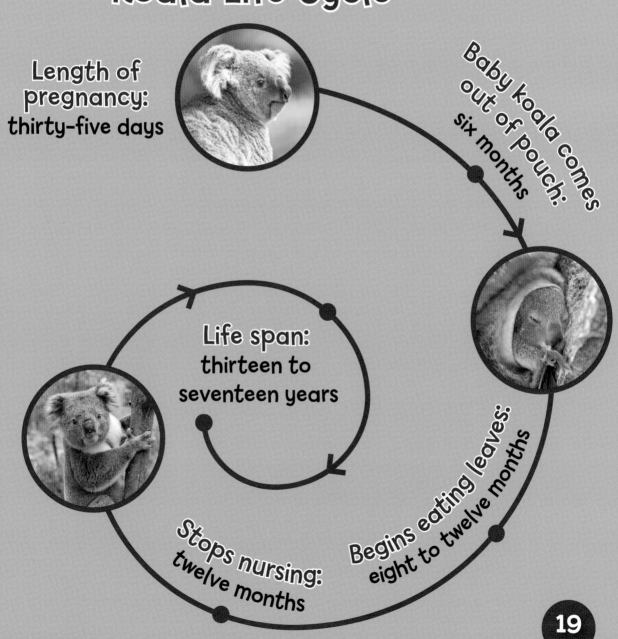

Length of pregnancy: thirty-five days

Baby koala comes out of pouch: six months

Life span: thirteen to seventeen years

Begins eating leaves: eight to twelve months

Stops nursing: twelve months

Habitat in Focus

- Wild koalas live only in Australia. Australia's habitat includes the type of trees koalas need to live.

- Kangaroos and wombats are other animals found only in Australia's habitat.

- Forests in Australia where koalas live are shrinking. People are cutting down the trees. Koalas are in danger of losing the trees they rely on for food.

Fun Facts

- Koalas spend most of the day sleeping. They move around and eat mostly at night.

- Koalas each have unique fingerprints, just like people!

- Many people call koalas bears. But koalas are actually a kind of animal called a marsupial. Marsupials mostly live in Australia and have pouches for their babies.

- A koala's scientific name is *Phascolarctos cinereus.* That means roughly "ash-gray pouch bear."

Glossary

cling: to hold tight

digest: to break down food inside the body

eucalyptus: a type of tree that grows naturally in western Australia

joey: a baby koala

pap: a substance mother koalas give to joeys to help with digestion

22

Further Reading

Australian Koala Foundation: Koalas for Kids
https://www.savethekoala.com/about-koalas /koalas-kids

Fishman, Jon M. *Meet a Baby Wombat*. Minneapolis: Lerner Publications, 2018.

Gregory, Josh. *Koalas*. New York: Children's Press, 2016.

National Geographic Kids: Koala
http://kids.nationalgeographic.com/animals /koala/#koala-closeup-tree.jpg

Owings, Lisa. *Learning about Australia*. Minneapolis: Lerner Publications, 2016.

San Diego Zoo Kids: Koala
http://kids.sandiegozoo.org/animals/mammals /koala

Index

Photo Acknowledgments

The images in this book are used with the permission of: © Suzi Eszterhas/Minden Pictures, pp. 2, 9, 10, 12, 19 (middle); © Arco Images GmbH/Alamy, p. 4; © D. Parer and E. Parer-CookMax/Minden Pictures, p. 5; © Roland Seitre/naturepl.com, pp. 6, 8; © iStockphoto.com/markrhiggins, p. 7; © Roland Seitre/Minden Pictures, p. 8; © VPC Animals Photo/Alamy, p. 11; © European Pressphoto Agency B.V./Alamy, p. 13; © iStockphoto.com/Andras Deak, p. 14; © imageBROKER/Alamy, pp. 15, 20; © Tui De Roy/Minden Pictures, p. 16; © Viktor Cap/Alamy, p. 17; © Gerry Pearce/Alamy, p. 18; © Gerard Lacz/Animals Animals, pp. 19 (top), 22; © blickwinkel/Alamy, p. 19 (bottom).

Front cover: apple2499/Shutterstock.com.

Main body text set in Billy Infant regular 28/36. Typeface provided by SparkType.